AIR

HOW TO USE YOUR SD-X READER WITH THIS BOOK

This highly interactive book lets you explore history and science in an interactive format. You can read the book and study the photographs and illustrations, but a touch of the SD-X Reader adds in-depth audio information, word definitions, and learning games to the page.

1. **Press the Power button to turn the SD-X Reader on or off. The LED will light up when the SD-X Reader is on.**

2. **Touch the volume buttons found on this page or on the Table of Contents page to adjust the volume.**

3. **Touch photographs and illustrations to hear additional information. Page headers and words or phrases that are in a different size or color than the surrounding text often provide a definition or more information.**

4. **As you explore the page, you'll encounter games and quizzes. Touch the text or image that started the game to stop playing.**

5. **After two minutes of inactivity, the Reader will beep and go to sleep.**

6. **If the batteries are low, the Reader will beep twice and the LED will start blinking. Replace the batteries by following the instructions on the next page. The SD-X Reader uses two AAA batteries.**

7. **To use headphones or earbuds, plug them into the headphone jack on the bottom of the SD-X Reader.**

CHANGE THE VOLUME WITH THESE BUTTONS

UP   DOWN

Battery Information
Interactive Pen includes 2 replaceable AAA batteries (UM-4 or LR03).

Battery Installation
1. Open battery door with small flat-head or Phillips screwdriver.
2. Install new batteries according to +/- polarity. If batteries are not installed properly, the device will not function.
3. Replace battery door; secure with small screw.

Battery Safety
Batteries must be replaced by adults only. Properly dispose of used batteries. Do not dispose of batteries in fire; batteries may explode or leak. See battery manufacturer for disposal recommendations. Do not mix alkaline, standard (carbon-zinc), or rechargeable (nickel-cadmium) batteries. Do not mix old and new batteries. Only recommended batteries of the same or equivalent type should be used. Remove weakened or dead batteries. Never short-circuit the supply terminals. Non-rechargeable batteries are not to be recharged. Do not use rechargeable batteries. If batteries are swallowed, in the USA, promptly see a doctor and have the doctor phone 1-202-625-3333 collect. In other countries, have the doctor call your local poison control center. Batteries should be changed when sounds mix, distort, or become otherwise unintelligible as batteries weaken. The electrostatic discharge may interfere with the sound module. If this occurs, please simply restart the product.

In Europe, the dustbin symbol indicates that batteries, rechargeable batteries, button cells, battery packs, and similar materials must not be discarded in household waste. Batteries containing hazardous substances are harmful to the environment and to health. Please help to protect the environment from health risks by telling your children to dispose of batteries properly and by taking batteries to local collection points. Batteries handled in this manner are safely recycled.

Warning: Changes or modifications to this unit not expressly approved by the party responsible for compliance could void the user's authority to operate the equipment.

NOTE: This equipment has been tested and found to comply with the limits for a Class B digital device, pursuant to Part 15 of the FCC Rules. These limits are designed to provide reasonable protection against harmful interference in a residential installation. This equipment generates, uses, and can radiate radio frequency energy and, if not installed and used in accordance with the instructions, may cause harmful interference to radio communications. However, there is no guarantee that interference will not occur in a particular installation. If this equipment does cause harmful interference to radio or television reception, which can be determined by turning the equipment off and on, the user is encouraged to try to correct the interference by one or more of the following measures: Reorient or relocate the receiving antenna. Increase the separation between the equipment and receiver. Connect the equipment into an outlet on a circuit different from that to which the receiver is connected. Consult the dealer or an experienced radio TV technician for help.

Cover art: Shutterstock.com

Interior art: NASA; Shutterstock.com; Smithsonian Institution; page 5, Orville Wright's camera, from Dayton History

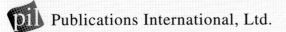 Publications International, Ltd.

Customer service: customer_service@pubint.com

ISBN: 978-1-68022-383-5

Manufactured in China.

8 7 6 5 4 3 2 1

CONTENTS

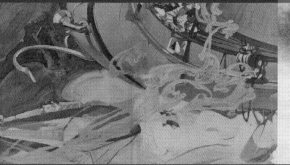
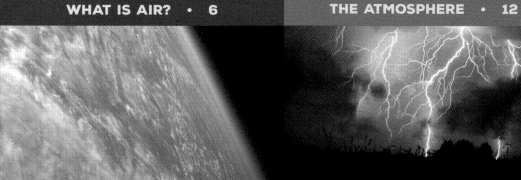

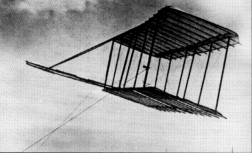

CHANGE THE VOLUME WITH THESE BUTTONS

UP   DOWN

AMERICAN AIR

Everywhere we look, science is there. Whether it is the ground we walk on, the water we drink, or the skies that we gaze upon, our world is shaped by science. The United States has long strived to increase humanity's understanding of the complex nature of scientific principles and properties in every context — from events that affect our daily lives to those that shape the fate of the universe. The Smithsonian plays a fundamental role in understanding the nature of the universe.

> "The worth and importance of the Institution is not to be estimated by what it accumulates within the walls of its building but by what it sends forth to the world."
> – Joseph Henry

ROOM TO IMPROVE

Joseph Henry was a physicist and the first Smithsonian Secretary. His legacy includes a wide array of things named in his honor, including a laboratory, a university teaching position, ships, and even a mountain range. He published articles on a wide variety of subjects, including electromagnetism, optics, acoustics, astrophysics, molecular forces, and magnetic fields, but his reputation was built on his work in basic and applied electromagnetism, like lightning. Henry also created the group of weather watchers who eventually became the National Weather Service.

BELL WEATHER

Alexander Graham Bell pursued a number of lines of investigation that eventually resulted in his inventing the telephone. He decided to introduce himself to Joseph Henry in 1875 during a trip to Washington. As he wrote in a letter to his parents, Bell wanted to "explain all the experiments, and ascertain what was new and what was old." Henry was 50 years older than 27-year-old Bell.

Bell wanted to know whether he should publish his research at once, or keep working on the problem himself. Henry advised him to work it out himself, calling it the "germ of a great invention." When Bell said he didn't have enough knowledge to overcome some of the mechanical difficulties, Henry simply replied, "GET IT."

THE WRIGHT STUFF

Have you ever wanted to know how an airplane flies? Or why you become "weightless" in space? Wilbur Wright wrote to the Smithsonian Institution on May 30, 1899. He believed that human flight was possible and asked for help with research. The Smithsonian's mission to support scientific research helped pave the way for the first airplane.

SCIENCE IN THE AIR

The Earth is blanketed in air. Humans need air to survive. Air is a mixture of different gases — about 78% nitrogen, 21% oxygen, and about 1% other gases. These gases make air a fluid, like water. Air is "stuff", as it has molecules that give it mass. Because air has mass, it is pulled down by gravity. Air is not just empty space—it has substance, or mass. Air has molecules that are constantly moving. Flight begins with air in motion. Without air, balloons and birds and airplanes couldn't fly.

TRUE OR FALSE

TRUE

FALSE

IS AIR REALLY THERE?

Air takes up space because it is made of particles. Gravity pulls on these particles and keeps them near Earth. This is why we have an atmosphere and why we are able to breathe. The density, or thickness, of air changes the farther away you get from Earth. The higher you go above Earth's surface the less air there is until there is none left!

AIR IS STUFF

Air composition is basically the same everywhere on the surface of the Earth: it's approximately 79% nitrogen, 20% oxygen, 1% a mix of lots of other stuff. Since it has mass, or stuff, it also has volume.

The composition of the atmosphere changes constantly and depends on the season, weather, time of day, latitude, longitude, elevation, and geography. In addition to gases, the atmosphere contains extras such as smoke, dust, acid droplets, and pollen.

Air composition can also vary due to pollutants. Some places have more pollutants in the air than others, and these pollutants can be different, too. Some other planets have atmospheres, but they are not all made of the same gasses that make up Earth's atmosphere.

AIR IS A FLUID

Fluids are states of matter that tend to flow around objects or take the shape of their container. Earth's gravity holds air to its surface, so we are all submerged in a "sea" of air.

AIR IS UNDER PRESSURE

Since air is invisible we easily forget that it is all around us. The weight of the air is constantly pushing against us, but it feels more like pressure than weight since it pushes from all sides. This all-around push is a force called air pressure. The pressure of the air in your lungs and in other spaces inside your body balances the pressure of the air around you.

AIR HAS HEAT ENERGY

When you have a gas, like air, you have molecules that are only interacting with each other when they bump into each other. They simply float around, minding their own business.

TRUE OR FALSE

 TRUE    FALSE

7

HOW IS AIR LIKE WATER?

ONE MILE RIVER BETWEEN LINDEMAN AND BENNETT

CHANGING SPEEDS

Air is a fluid, and at slow speeds it behaves like water. Fluids, such as air and water, change speed as they flow between and around things. When air moves through a narrow channel or around an object, it speeds up. As it speeds up, its pressure drops and it pushes less. Freely flowing water does not compress easily. Instead, it speeds up as the channel narrows. Water also speeds up as it moves around an object, such as a rock in a river.

FLOWING CURRENTS

In the early 1700s, a Swiss mathematician named Daniel Bernoulli made a discovery. He noticed that when flowing air or water changed its speed, its pressure also changed.

There are currents in the air. Differences in air pressure can actually create currents in the air, and we can feel this as wind. Birds and gliders use these currents to remain airborne while using little or none of their own energy.

DIFFERENT DENSITIES

Density is a measure of how much mass is "packed" into a given space. Many processes are caused by differences in the densities between fluids and solids.

WATER

A boat can float on water because there is air inside the boat that makes the boat less dense than the water. A hot-air balloon can float because hot air is less dense than the colder air around the balloon. If the object cannot float, then the **buoyancy** is less than the object's weight.

AIR

TRUE OR FALSE

TRUE

FALSE

WHAT CAN AIR CARRY?

The sun, the earth, and the rest of the solar system formed from a cloud of dust and gas 4.6 billion years ago. Earth's atmosphere has just the right amounts of oxygen, carbon dioxide and ozone to support life. The air is never still. Stirred by the sun's heat, air moves across the Earth in vast currents. In its travels, air picks up interesting stuff, from small amounts of gases or chemicals to particles of dust, smoke, or bacteria and other tiny organisms.

Anything that's in the air moves with it. Atmosphere's hitchhikers can travel thousands of miles, changing air quality and transforming life across continents.

VOLCANOES CHANGE WEATHER

Erupting volcanoes blast out fine particles known as **aerosols** that can circle the globe, blocking sunlight and dropping temperatures worldwide.

GOBI DESERT DUST BLANKET

Dust from the Gobi Desert in Mongolia is rich in iron. Every spring it travels over China, the Korean Peninsula, and Japan to the North Pacific.

AFRICAN DUST TRAVELS FAR

Among the 80 experiments performed on the space shuttle Columbia before its tragic loss in 2003, Israeli astronaut Ilan Ramon tracked and measured desert dust over North Africa, the Mediterranean Sea, and North America.

SMOKE CLOUDS OUR SKY AND LUNGS

"Smoke is made up small particles, gases, and water vapor. Water vapor makes up the majority of smoke. It's a good idea to avoid breathing smoke if you can help it. Smoke also can travel long distances, so fires in other areas can affect smoke levels in your area."

TRUE OR **FALSE**

WE AFFECT THE AIR

People have been affecting the atmosphere for tens of thousands of years. Although a few important people complained about polluted air, no one paid much attention. Human impact on the atmosphere skyrocketed during the Industrial Revolution of the 19th century.

AIR IS THE ATMOSPHERE

The atmosphere has been changing since Earth began. Once living things learned how to do **photosynthesis**—perhaps 2.7 billion years ago—they began to remake the atmosphere. Ever since then, living things and Earth's atmosphere have worked together. As far as we know, the relationship is unique to Earth.

about 380–500 km

about 80–100 km

about 50–60 km

about 6–18 km

EXOSPHERE

THERMOSPHERE

MESOSPHERE

STRATOSPHERE

TROPOSPHERE

Temperature decreases with height, about -50 °C (poles), -80 °C (equator)

Temperature increases with height, about 0 °C

Temperature decreases with height, about -100 °C

Temperature increases with height, about 1500 °C

TROPOPAUSE

OZONOSPHERE

STRATOPAUSE

MESOPAUSE

THERMOPAUSE

IONOSPHERE

THE DAWN OF THE OXYGEN AGE

The chemical mix of the atmosphere changes constantly and depends on the season, weather, time of day, latitude, longitude, elevation, and geography. In the 4.6 billion years of Earth's history, the composition of the atmosphere has changed from a hazy, unfamiliar mix to today's mostly blue skies.

When Earth formed 4.6 billion years ago from a hot mix of gases and solids, it had almost no atmosphere. The surface was **molten**. After about half a billion years, Earth's surface cooled and solidified enough for water to collect on it.

The atmosphere of the planet Earth is a layer of oxygen and nitrogen gas, held to the Earth by our planet's gravity. It provides air for us to breathe and creates pressure on our skin. Some other planets have atmospheres, but they are not all made of the same gasses that make up Earth's atmosphere.

TROPOSPHERE

STRATOSPHERE

MESOSPHERE

THERMOSPHERE

EXOSPHERE

TRUE OR FALSE

T F

There was no oxygen gas on Earth. Oxygen was only in compounds such as water. Simple, living cells did not need oxygen to live. Instead they made energy out of sulfur and other elements. Life and Earth's atmosphere evolved together. About two billion years ago, the sky turned blue.

HISTORY IN THE AIR

For billions of years, our atmosphere has been:
- A shield against bombarding meteorites
- A shade against destructive ultraviolet radiation
- A blanket against the cold

Oxygen made up 20 percent of the atmosphere—about today's level—beginning around 350 million years ago. All **aerobic** organisms use oxygen to release energy from the proteins, fats, and carbohydrates in food. This process is called metabolism.

We inherit the ability to use oxygen from ancient life that evolved ways to survive more and more oxygen in earth's atmosphere. Without it, the oxygen would have poisoned these life forms. For other organisms, oxygen was poisonous after all, and they were forced into extreme airless habitats or into extinction.

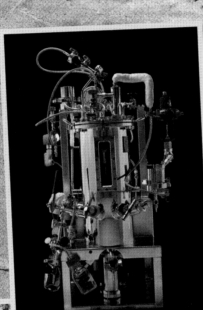

During most of the past 290 million years, Earth was much warmer than it is now. Scientists understand that changes in the atmosphere affect Earth's climate. Between 200 and 45 million years ago, winters were warmer around the globe. In these warm climates, many types of plants and animals lived at the North and South Poles.

Human activity is changing two of our atmosphere's protective duties. The ozone layer—the part of the stratosphere layer that protects us from the sun's ultraviolet radiation—has deteriorated. The rising level of "greenhouse gases" in the atmosphere is raising Earth's temperature faster than at any time in the past.

Most meteorites burn up before they reach the ground. If they didn't, space **debris** would fall to Earth's surface like rain. A few meteorites, however, are too big to burn up completely, and they strike Earth.

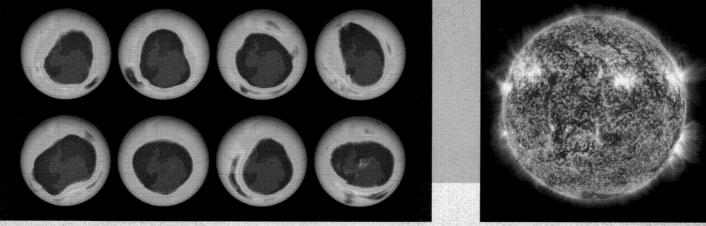

Greenhouse gases are made up of at least two atoms. Bonds between the atoms absorb heat that radiates from Earth's surface and would otherwise be lost in space. Greenhouse gases keep Earth warm much as a greenhouse keeps plants warm in winter.

Human activity increases the amount of greenhouse gases in the atmosphere—mainly carbon dioxide from the burning of fossil fuels. The extra greenhouse gas may be trapping too much heat, raising Earth's temperatures. Although Earth's average temperature naturally changes, the current rapid rise in temperatures—global warming—is potentially harmful to life on Earth.

TRUE OR FALSE

T F

THE AIR OUT WHERE?

VENUS

Venus is about the same size as Earth. Venus rotates in a backward direction. Because Venus is closer to the Sun than Earth and has a very thick atmosphere, the surface temperature is as much as 900° F. Venus has a thick atmosphere of carbon dioxide. Atmospheric pressure at the surface is 90 times that of Earth.

MERCURY

Mercury's atmosphere is so thin that it is barely detectable.

MARS

For at least the past two billion years, Mars has been a cold desert, where wind and dust carve the landscape. Unlike Venus, whose thick clouds hide its surface, Mars showed light and dark markings with its changing seasons. Martian rocks show there was probably an ancient magnetic field, like the one Earth and some other planets have, that vanished a long time ago. Water-ice clouds, formed as moist air rises and cools, are almost a daily occurrence around Olympus, the tallest volcano on Mars or anywhere in the solar system. Mars today is a cold, dry desert with an atmosphere so thin that any surface water evaporates or freezes.

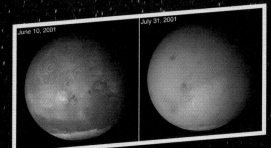

June 10, 2001 | July 31, 2001

TRUE or FALSE

False
True

16

At any given moment, many chemicals form, break apart, and re-form in the air we breathe. While our ocean of air is very big, changes in a tiny amount of our air can also change the delicate balance of life on Earth. But what about other planets in our solar system? Each planet in the solar system has seasons. Earth has four seasons. What is the same about the seasons on other planets? Only their names: winter, spring, summer, and fall. The seasons are different on each planet. On Venus, seasons are short. On Saturn, a season can last for seven years. And on Mercury, you can't even tell when one season ends and the next one begins.

JUPITER

Stripes of clouds have long been seen on Jupiter, and the reddish area below the equator, the Great Red Spot, has been known to exist for more than 300 years. Jupiter's atmosphere contains many belts and storm systems with wind speeds up to 250 miles per hour.

SATURN

Like Jupiter, winds in Saturn's atmosphere move both west and east, creating storms where they pass each other. White clouds in the atmosphere appear to leave a trail of smaller clouds behind them.

URANUS

Uranus' axis of rotation is tilted nearly 98°, almost perpendicular to its orbit. This changes the seasons and days on Uranus. At times, the north pole points toward the Sun. At other times the south pole does.

NEPTUNE

Like Earth's atmosphere, Neptune's has clouds and storm systems that revolve around the planet — but with wind speeds of 700 miles per hour and clouds of frozen methane instead of water. The "Great Dark Spot" is a storm system that resembles Jupiter's Red Spot.

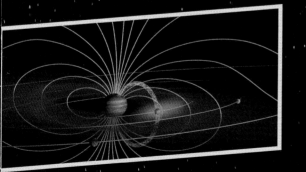

17

UPLIFTING *FORCES*

Understanding how things fly begins by learning about the **Four Forces of Flight**. When an airplane flies, the wing is designed to provide enough **Lift** to overcome the airplane's **Weight**, while the engine provides enough **Thrust** to overcome **Drag** and move the airplane forward. And the **Thrust** of a rocket engine overcomes the **Weight** of the object to move the rocket forward.

THE FOUR FORCES

LIFT

WEIGHT

THRUST

DRAG

LIFT

THRUST

DRAG

NI538C

WEIGHT

TRUE
OR FALSE?

THRUST

WEIGHT

BIRDS ARE BUILT TO FLY

Birds inspired our first attempts to fly, but our progress was limited until we learned that we could not fly like them.

Birds use the same four forces of flight as airplanes to fly.
And many birds have hollow or honeycombed bones, which are strong but lightweight.

RISE
ABOVE IT

Understanding gravity and air is key to flight. To rise above it all, you have to face some facts: You must grapple with gravity no matter how or where you fly, because gravity is everywhere—you can't escape it. Gravity holds us to the surface of the Earth and keeps our atmosphere wrapped around our planet.

Hot-air balloons and blimps can float in the air thanks to Buoyancy, an upward force that the air exerts on them.

BUOYANCY

AERODYNAMICS

Aerodynamics is the study of forces and the resulting motion of objects through the air. Everything moving through the air (including airplanes, rockets, and birds) is affected by aerodynamics.

WHAT A DRAG

Drag is a force that tries to slow something down. It makes it hard for an object to move. It is harder to walk or run through water than through air. That is because water causes more drag than air. The shape of an object also changes the amount of drag. Most round surfaces have less drag than flat ones. Narrow surfaces usually have less drag than wide ones. The more air that hits a surface, the more drag it makes.

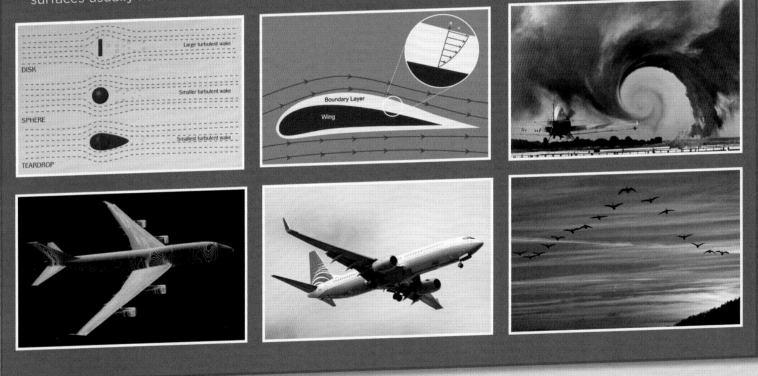

As an airplane moves through the air, its wings cause changes in the speed and pressure of the air moving past them. These changes result in the upward force called lift. Studying the motion of air around an object allows us to measure the forces of lift, which allows an aircraft to overcome gravity, and drag, which is the resistance an aircraft "feels" as it moves through the air.

TRUE OR FALSE

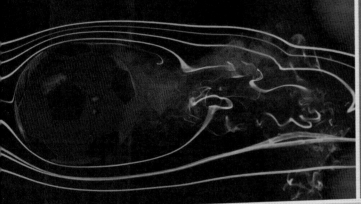

STREAMLINING

A streamlined body is a shape that lowers the friction drag between a fluid, like air and water, and an object moving through that fluid. Many animals, such as birds and dolphins, and many machines, such as airplanes and submarines, have streamlined bodies to reduce friction drag as they move through either air or water

DRAG CAN HELP

A parachute is a folding, umbrella-shaped piece of light fabric used for many things but especially to make a safe descent from an airplane. Some parachutes use slots and holes to steer the parachute.

GET A MOVE ON

Thrust is the push that moves something forward. For an aircraft to keep moving forward, it must have more thrust than drag. A small airplane might get its thrust from a propeller. A larger airplane might get its thrust from jet engines. A glider does not have thrust. It can only fly until the drag causes it to slow down and land.

PROPELLERS

Think of a propeller as a spinning wing. Like a wing, it produces lift, but forward—a force we refer to as thrust. In order for a propeller blade to spin, it usually needs the help of an engine. A ship's propellers create thrust in water in much the same way an airplane's propellers create thrust in air.

HELICOPTERS

Many people, including Leonardo da Vinci, drew plans for helicopters. Helicopters come closer to achieving the freedom of bird flight that humanity has always wanted. But helicopters can't get the speeds and abilities of airplanes doing the same jobs.

A helicopter's spinning blades create thrust like a large propeller, but the thrust is up instead of forward.

THERE'S THE RUB

An airplane has **friction** drag. Friction drag is the resistance of the air along the surface of the plane. The air rubs along the plane and actually slows it down. A fast aircraft also squeezes the air in front of it and makes the air's temperature go up.

SPACE SHUTTLE

The space shuttle weighed about 4.5 million pounds when it lifted off, and 2.9 million pounds of that was propellant.

When the shuttle returned to Earth, it glided on a pair of wings and landed on a runway.

JET ENGINES

There are three types of engines that power most flying machines: piston engines, jet engines and rocket engines. Engines burn fuel to create hot, expanding gasses that make thrust.

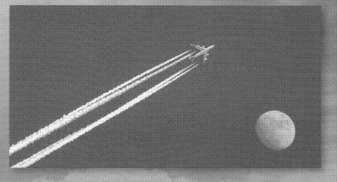

Sound is a type of wave that travels through air, water, and more. The speed of sound in the air mainly depends on temperature. A moving airplane makes a wave similar to a sound wave. As an airplane approaches the speed of sound, anyone in the wave's path will hear a **sonic boom**

TRUE or **FALSE** **T** **F**

ROCKETS

Rockets (and jet engines) work much like a balloon filled with air. If you fill a balloon with air and hold it closed, the pressure inside the balloon is slightly higher than the surrounding atmosphere. But if you let go, the balloon flies forward. Thrust is a force pushing the balloon forward.

Jet engines and rockets work on the same idea. The main difference is that rockets carry their own oxygen so they can work in space where there's no air. Jets take air in one way and shoot it out the other way, but rockets only shoot air out.

A rocket needs lots of fuel plus the oxygen needed to burn the fuel. The oxygen weighs more than the fuel. The fuel and oxygen together are called the propellant. The rocket must lift the spacecraft plus the weight of its propellant. The propellant to get into Earth orbit is usually at least 20 times more than the spacecraft and cargo it carries.

Since the dawn of history, from the Greek myth of Icarus to the flying machines of Leonardo da Vinci, humankind has dreamt of flight. That dream became reality when the hot air balloon was invented in 1783 by the Montgolfier brothers.

Inspired by watching clothes billow over an open fire, the Montgolfier brothers experimented with fabric bags filled with heated air.

FANTASTIC WORLDS

Travel to the surface of the moon, the center of the earth, and the depths of the ocean — to the fantastic worlds of fiction inspired by 19th-century discovery and invention. We took to the air, charted remote corners of the earth, and harnessed the power of steam and electricity. We began unlocking the secrets of the natural world.

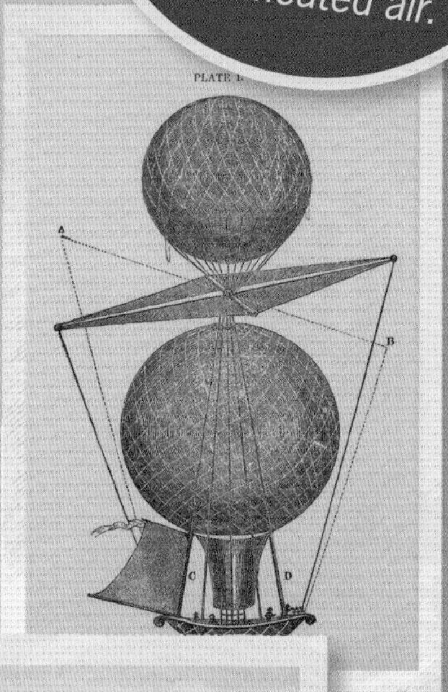

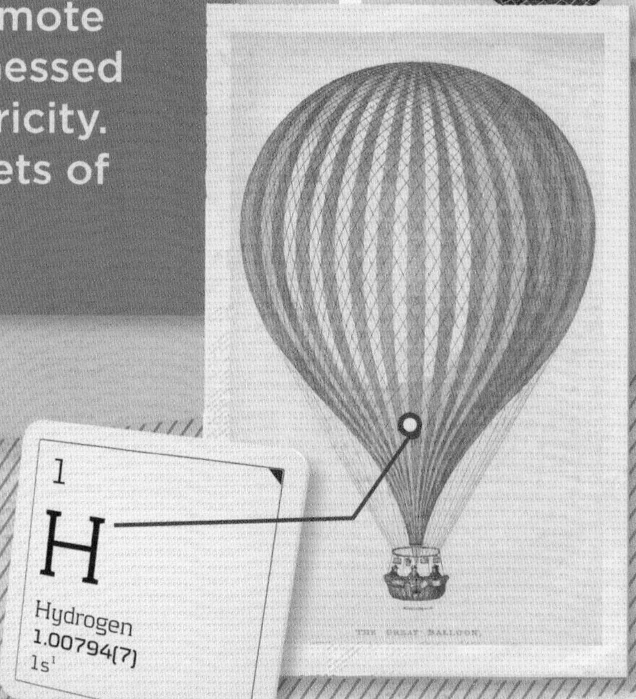

TRUE
OR FALSE?

1

H

Hydrogen
1.00794(7)
$1s^1$

As the 19th century progressed, fantastic airships became a mainstay of fiction. Intrepid travelers flew beyond the gravitational pull of the Earth to Mars. Ships sailed from the ocean into the air.

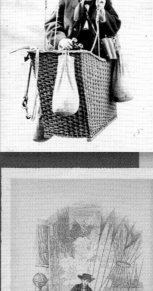

"The great problem is at length solved. The air, as well as the earth and the ocean, has been subdued by science, and will become a common and convenient highway for mankind. The Atlantic has been actually crossed in a balloon..."

— Edgar Allan Poe,
"The Balloon Hoax"

EARLY DREAMS
OF FLIGHT

The Wright brothers weren't actually the first people to try to fly, though they managed to think of flight differently than other scientists before them.

CENTURIES AHEAD OF HIS TIME

In 1506, Leonardo da Vinci turned more and more to scientific observation rather than painting. He filled notebooks with data and drawings, including the flight of birds, leading to designs for human flight. It was only after 1800 that the record of his intellectual and technical accomplishments, the thousands of pages of writings and drawings, began to surface. Leonardo lived a fifteenth century life, but a vision of the modern world spread before his mind's eye.

TRUE OR FALSE?

Englishman Sir George Cayley was a turning point in the history of aviation. Cayley was the first to do flight research grounded in the scientific method.

THE FLYING MAN

The most important experimenter before the Wright brothers was the German glider pioneer Otto Lilienthal. Between 1891 and 1896, he built and flew a series of highly successful full-size gliders.

WHO WERE WILBER & ORVILL?

Orville and Wilbur Wright invented the world's first airplane. Their fame and popular stature is extraordinary, but their personal story is largely unknown. How did two men, working essentially alone and with little formal scientific training, solve a problem so complex and demanding as heavier-than-air flight, which had defied better-known experimenters for centuries? Certainly the brothers were talented, but the true answer also lies in their background and early experiences.

THE BROTHERS' EARLY LIVES

Wilbur was self-confident, controlled, and of steady demeanor—"never rattled in thought or temper," as his father described him. Highly intelligent, he was a voracious reader, a talented writer, and a gifted speaker. Outgoing when circumstances required, he could also isolate himself and shut out the world when he chose.

Orville showed an interest in technology and science early in life. He was always performing experiments and dismantling things to find out how they worked. He fit the stereotype of the budding inventor far more than Wilbur.

A PAIR FOR THE PRESSES

Orville began a printing business as a teenager, in which Wilbur later joined him. They did job-printing and published several short-lived local newspapers.

The close and productive team that created the first airplane formed during this period.

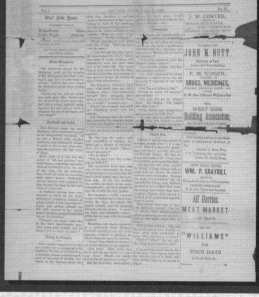

WHAT WAS NEXT?

In designing their airplane, the Wrights drew upon a number of bicycle concepts:
- *The central importance of balance and control.*
- *The need for strong but light structures.*
- *The chain-and-sprocket system for propulsion.*
- *Concerns regarding wind resistance and aerodynamic shape of the operator.*

DAYTON IN THE 1890S

The Wright brothers lived a happy and contented life in Dayton. They were proud to be from Ohio and believed that growing up there gave them certain advantages in life.

Bird's Eye View from Conover Building, looking South, Dayton, Ohio.

TRUE OR FALSE?

A BICYCLE BUSINESS

At the height of the bicycle boom in the 1890s, more than 300 companies were producing over a million bicycles per year. The brothers purchased bicycles in the spring of 1892. Wilbur preferred long country rides, while Orville enjoyed racing and considered himself a "scorcher" on the track. Surprisingly, no photographs exist of Wilbur or Orville on or with a bicycle.

WRIGHT CYCLE Co.

Repair Departrment.

We guarantee all work; but complaint must be made promptly.

Storage will be charged on all wheels not called for in ten days.

KEEP THIS CARD.

No. 1039

The Wright brothers' major technical activity before flight was bicycle repair and manufacture. The Wrights' growing local reputation as skillful cyclists and mechanics led to many requests from friends to fix their bicycles. In 1893 they capitalized on the situation and opened a small rental and repair shop. The business not only provided their livelihood, but also funded their aeronautical experiments.

INVENTING A FLYING MACHINE

Between 1899 and 1905, the Wright brothers conducted a program of **AERONAUTICAL** research and experimentation that led to the first successful powered airplane in 1903 and a refined, practical flying machine two years later. All successful airplanes since then have incorporated the basic design elements of the 1903 Wright Flyer.

MAKING CONNECTIONS

In the 1890s aviation was a wide-open field of study. a community of technically trained people interested in flight had evolved. They had knowledge that represented the first real steps toward human flight.

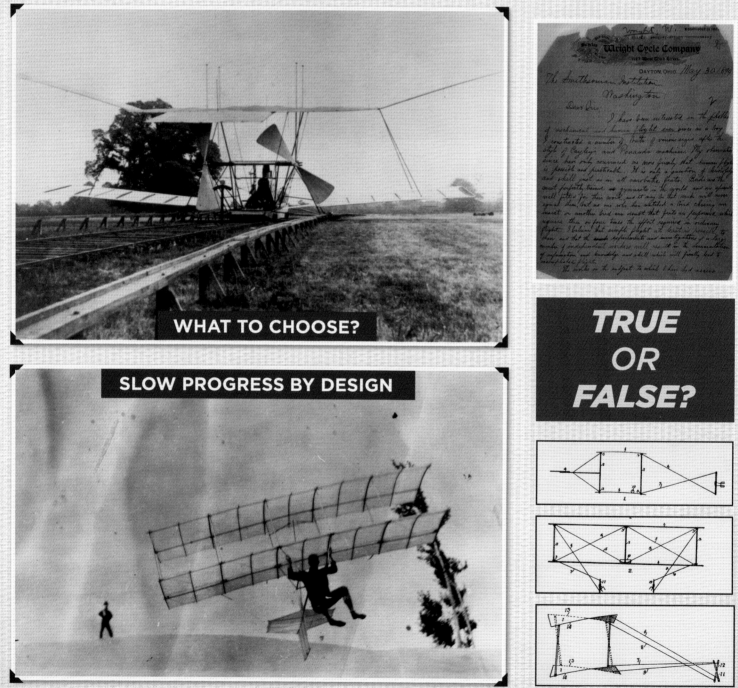

WHAT TO CHOOSE?

SLOW PROGRESS BY DESIGN

TRUE OR FALSE?

GO FLY A KITE

The Wrights' first aircraft, a biplane kite with a 5-foot wingspan, was built in July 1899. The kite responded quickly and precisely to Wilbur's commands. The Wrights began designing a full-size, piloted glider. It was one thing to design a set of wings for a small kite, quite another to build a large, heavy glider, climb aboard, and launch oneself into the air.

THE GOOD . . .

AND THE BAD.

A WING AND A PRAYER

They returned to Kitty Hawk in 1901 to test the new glider. To increase lift on their next glider, they increased the size of the wings and the curvature of the **AIRFOIL**. The results were discouraging. The new glider performed worse than the 1900 craft.

After building and testing a small **WIND TUNNEL**, the Wright brothers completed a larger, more sophisticated one in October 1901.

Rather than risk life and limb on a large, heavy, untried powered flying machine, Wilbur and Orville decided to build one more glider.

THE FINAL COUNTDOWN

Buoyant over the success of their 1902 glider, the Wright brothers were no longer content to merely add to the growing body of aeronautical knowledge; they were going to invent the airplane. Still, they recognized that much hard work lay ahead. This year things were different. They were going to fly an airplane.

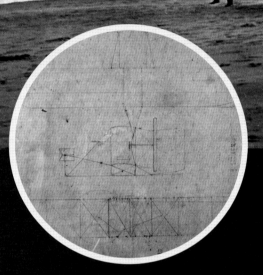

"Our new machine is a very great improvement over anything anyone has built. Everything is so much more satisfactory that we now believe that the flying problem is really nearing its solution." — Wilbur Wright, 1902

DESIGNING THE FLYER

To design their first powered airplane, which they simply called the Flyer, the Wrights returned to their wind tunnel data. To carry the weight of an engine, propellers, and added reinforcement, they had to increase the wing area to more than **500 SQUARE FEET**.

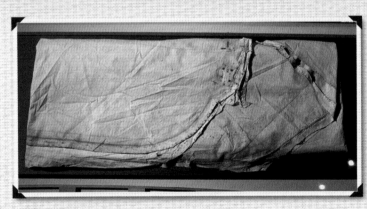

"After a while they shook hands, and we couldn't help notice how they held on to each other's hand, sort o'like they hated to let go; like two folks parting who weren't sure they'd ever see each other again." — John T. Daniels, Kitty Hawk lifesaving crewman, recalling the moments before the first flight

Orville WRIGHT

TRUE OR FALSE?

TRIUMPH!

On December 14, three months after arriving at Kitty Hawk, the Wrights were finally ready to give their creation a try. They tossed a coin to determine which brother would make the first attempt. Wilbur won.

With damage repaired, the Flyer was again ready for flight on December 17. At 10:35 a.m., the Flyer lifted off with Orville at the controls. The Flyer darted up and down as it sailed slowly over the sand, coming to rest with a thud 120 feet from where it had taken off. The flight was short—only 12 seconds—but it was a true flight nevertheless. A human had flown. On its final flight, Wilbur steadied the airplane for an impressive 852-foot trip in 59 seconds. The Wright Flyer was capable of sustained, controlled flight.

THE AERIAL AGE BEGINS

By the fall of 1905, the Wright brothers' experimental period ended. On October 5, Wilbur made a flight of 39 minutes and a total distance of 24 1/2 miles. Human flight was so significant and revolutionary a breakthrough that its influence went well beyond the aeronautical community. Today Wilbur and Orville Wright are part of the national cultural identity, and the Wright Flyer is an icon of ingenuity and technical creativity.

NAVIGATING IN THE AIR

Navigation is the art and science of getting from point "A" to point "B" in the shortest time without losing your way. In the early days of air flight, the tools to help with flight had not been invented yet, so pilots did their best using their eyes and other senses. Today, navigation is a science and advanced equipment is standard on most aircraft.

CHALLENGES OF SEA NAVIGATION

In 1700, Europe's sailors and mapmakers knew only about half the Earth's surface with any detail. But uncharted seas were dangerous, and unpredictable air movements like strong winds and storms threw ships off course.

OUT OF THIN AIR

Finding position in the air was more difficult than at sea, and becoming lost often meant death. Early pilots on long flights faced great danger if they could not figure out exactly where they were—just like sailors from centuries before. But the tools sailors used at sea didn't work as well in the air. Airplanes moved many times faster than ships, so air navigators had to work faster to fix their position. Even minor miscalculations could result in much greater errors.

The type of navigation used depends on where the pilot is going, how long the flight will take, when the flight is scheduled to take off, the type of aircraft being flown, the on-board navigation equipment, the pilot's experience and education, and especially the expected weather.

Dead reckoning is the simplest means of navigating but the least accurate over long distances. Cloudy or stormy weather can prevent a pilot from seeing the needed landmarks like roads or rivers. Pilots may become confused and navigate off course. Pilots may also want to fly in areas without many people or towns where there are simply not many landmarks to use. Radio navigation became the main method of navigation because of its precision and ease of use.

CROSSING THE OCEAN

Many nations took on the challenge of navigating across the ocean by air. In peacetime, these achievements showed how far aviation had come in only a few years. Between the world wars, the United States and many European countries competed by setting new transoceanic records, establishing overseas airline service, and demonstrating military power. And as World War II began, the ability to cross oceans by air meant that no nation was safe from attack.

Many air navigation pioneers wanted to distinguish themselves from sea navigators. One way they tried to do so was to call air navigation "avigation" and air navigators "avigators." It did not catch on.

CELESTIAL NAVIGATION

RADIO NAVIGATION

DEAD RECKONING

TRUE or FALSE

T   F

HARD to NAVIGATE

Aviators made unprecedented long-distance flights. It was exciting but dangerous. Many people tried, and many died.

CHARLES LINDBERGH

Charles Lindbergh flew alone across the Atlantic in 1927, but that year included other record flights that presented far greater challenges. But the limitations of navigation technology often proved deadly. Even the relatively simple-seeming task of crossing the North Atlantic claimed many lives. These disasters marked a turning point in navigational systems.

In 1919 a New York hotel owner offered a $25,000 prize for the first nonstop flight between New York and Paris. Early in 1927, Charles Lindbergh found nine St. Louis investors to fund him to compete for the prize. Though not the first person to cross the Atlantic Ocean by air — over 100 had preceded him — Lindbergh flew alone and showed that transatlantic flight would soon be practical. Because he lacked any means for fixing position, his flight also illustrated that, until better navigational tools and techniques were developed, this type of flying could be a gamble. Indeed, many who attempted it perished.

Despite weather changes and extreme fatigue, Lindbergh reached the coast of Ireland within 3 miles of his planned course. But he knew that chance, not skill or equipment, had allowed such accuracy—winds during his flight had caused no significant drift.

FINDING A BETTER WAY

The problems of reliable air navigation experienced by Lindbergh and other aviators was finally addressed in the late 1920s by a few dedicated innovators who often worked with little official support to make improvements in dead reckoning and radio and celestial navigation equipment.

As Charles Lindbergh retired the Spirit of St. Louis to the Smithsonian Institution in 1928, he was planning even riskier oceanic flights. He knew his seat-of-the-pants approach to navigation was no longer enough. Lindbergh sought out the best navigation instructor he could find: U.S. Navy Lieutenant Commander Philip Van Horn Weems.

Weems' greatest legacy was influencing the air navigation programs of U.S. airlines and the military. His techniques became the standard for long-range navigation for three decades.

USING NEW TECHNOLOGY

While ships could carry reliable chronometers to time celestial observations, aviators needed smaller, lighter, and more accessible time pieces. Such clocks could be made, but at the cost of precision and accuracy. One solution was the use of radio broadcasts of time signals that allowed air navigators to accurately set their watches to the second.

While instructing Lindbergh, Weems used several new innovations, most of his own design. After this training, Lindbergh would never again fly long distances without having the latest in celestial navigation equipment. In 1933, Charles and Anne Morrow Lindbergh went on a five-month, four-continent flight tour from the North Atlantic to Europe, Africa, and South America. Charles and Anne demonstrated that long-range air navigation could be safe, practical, and reliable.

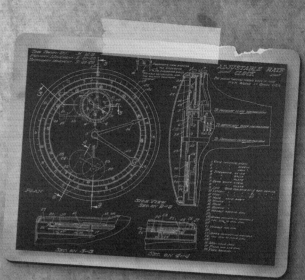

PIONEERS AND MISTAKES

Wiley Post, with Harold Gatty as navigator, circled the world in 1931, shattering previous records. Their plane, the Winnie Mae, served as a flying laboratory for many new technologies, including the new Weems System of Navigation.

During an around-the-world flight attempt in 1937, Amelia Earhart and her expert navigator, Fred Noonan, vanished in the South Pacific. Their disappearance served as warning to other aviators not to take navigation lightly.

"I believe that within two or three weeks work in celestial navigation and perhaps two or three months serious work with radio, you would be in a class almost by yourself."
– P. V. H. Weems to Amelia Earhart in 1937

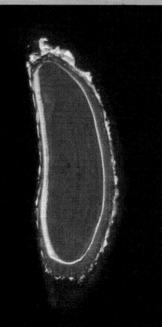

Their eastbound route led them into headwinds that cost them fuel. Clouds hampered their navigational sightings. Neither knew Morse code, critical for the ship-based radio direction finder system the Navy used to support their flight. The plane was poorly outfitted for navigation and long-range communication, and neither was well trained on the radio equipment they did have. Their flight required an effective blend of dead-reckoning, celestial navigation, and radio direction finding, but poor planning, inexperience, and circumstance compromised all three.

TRUE OR FALSE

WHAT IS SOUND?

Sound is waves transmitted through the air (or another substance) by molecules bumping into each other. When these sound waves reach your ear, they cause your ear drums to vibrate. Your brain "decodes" the vibrations into voices, music, and noises.

The movement of sound is affected by temperature, density and pressure. Since temperature, density and pressure all decrease with altitude, the speed of sound slows down the higher up you get.

THE SPEED OF SOUND

The speed of sound in the air mainly depends on temperature. At a typical sea level temperature, sound travels about 760 miles per hour. At high altitudes, where it is much colder, sound travels slower, about 660 miles per hour. Speeds faster than the speed of sound are known as supersonic.

PICTURING SOUND

Édouard-Léon Scott de Martinville invented the phonautograph, an instrument which scratched records of aerial sound waves on soot-blackened paper, not for playback, but for visual study. First patented in 1857 and updated many times, his design would influence the direction of sound studies. The phonautograph was the first device to imitate the structure and function of the human ear.

Alexander Graham Bell received the fundamental U.S. patent for the telephone and telephone system in 1876.

In the early 1870s, while teaching in Boston, Bell had been studying acoustics at the Institute of Technology (now MIT). His experiments there, especially working with a physician to construct a phonautograph based on the operation of the human ear, gave him the idea for the electric telephone and influenced his work on sound recording.

REPLAYING SOUND

Thomas Edison amazed the world in 1877 when he invented his "talking machine," the first instrument ever to record and play back sound.

Alexander Graham Bell and his colleagues made a wide range of sound experiments. Improving Thomas Edison's invention was their major goal. Their experiments led to commercial innovations—most notably the wax cylinder record and the graphophone, a machine to record and play back cylinders.

LEARNING FROM SOUND

The graphophone became a widely used dictation machine for business, eventually made and sold by the Dictaphone Corporation. Portable versions of machines for making cylinder recordings transformed the study of cultures in anthropology and folklore.

Many experimental recordings made between 1881 and 1885 were considered unplayable until recently. Over the past decade, sound scientists have recovered sound from recordings in a number of collections and a wide range of record formats and conditions. This work offers hope in preserving collections of early sound recordings around the world. A large amount of our cultural heritage has been captured on fragile or outdated recording media, and, without preservation, the content is not playable and in danger of being lost forever.

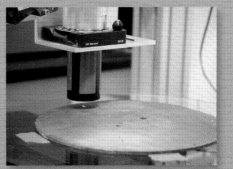

TRUE or FALSE

T **F**

THE ELECTRIC AIR

Electricity is simply the movement of charges. The electrons flowing through a wire carry a negative charge. A lightning bolt is the same idea, just without the wire.

Electricity is made by converting some form of energy into flowing electons. The type of power-plant used to make electricity depends on the source of energy, like wind, water, or nuclear reactions.

WHAT'S A LASER?

Ordinary light, like sunlight, is made up of many different wavelengths, or colors, of light. How is laser light different? First, the light from a laser contains exactly one color or wavelength rather than a lot of different wavelengths. Scientists say that laser light is "monochromatic," meaning of one color. Second, all the wavelengths are in phase. That is, they are all "waving" together, like a well-timed audience "wave" at a football game. All the high points and low points are lined up. And third, while light waves from ordinary sources (such as flashlights, lightbulbs, or the Sun) spread out in all directions, laser light waves all travel in the same direction, exactly parallel to one another. This means that laser light beams are very narrow and can be concentrated on one tiny spot.

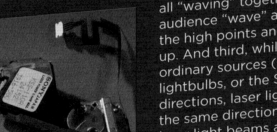

While astronomers were starting to use photography to capture light from celestial objects, they were also learning how to analyze light itself. They found that an object's spectrum, the rainbow of colors that forms when light passes through a prism, could tell them what the object was made of and how it moved. For example, as light passes through a gas, the gas soaks up certain colors, or wavelengths, of light.

The light from a laser in space would continue on forever unless it hit something. When you use a laser pointer, you only see a tiny spot across the room. But if you were looking at the spot even further away, it would be slightly bigger. If you go far enough away, the light will eventually spread out far enough to be undetectable — even in space.

WHAT'S A COMPASS?

The magnetic compass originated in China and was in use in Europe by the twelfth century. Pilots use a compass to determine direction when flying airplanes. Boaters, hikers, and hunters are examples of other people who rely on compasses. A compass is an instrument that aligns a free pivoting bar magnet (called the needle) in Earth's magnetic field.

LIQUID COMPASS

DRY CARD COMPASS

POCKET COMPASS

TELL-TALE COMPASS

HOW CAN HUMANS USE AIR TO MAKE POWER?

There are a many ways to produce electricity. Wind-mills convert energy into electricity. They use the energy of motion. Since no fuel is burned, no air pollution is produced. Wind is a renewable resources and we have a long history of harnessing this energy source.

But there are a limited number of suitable locations where the wind blows predictably. Even in such sites, turbines often have to be designed with special gearing so that the rotor will turn at a constant speed in spite of variable wind speeds. Some find less technical problems with installations that can turn a scenic ridge or pass into an ugly steel forest, or that can take a toll on birds.

TRUE or FALSE **T** **F**

41

CHANGING WEATHER, CHANGING CLIMATE

Nearly every scientific and social issue facing us today involves change: climate change, ecological change, cultural change. What forces drive these changes? What is the speed and mode of these changes? Are these changes natural or the result of human behavior? Are they to be feared or welcomed? How do we — and all life on this planet — adapt to these changes?

WHAT IS WEATHER?

In most places, weather can change from minute-to-minute, hour-to-hour, day-to-day, and season-to-season. There are really a lot of components to weather. Weather includes sunshine, rain, cloud cover, winds, hail, snow, sleet, freezing rain, flooding, blizzards, ice storms, thunderstorms, steady rains from a cold front or warm front, excessive heat, heat waves and more.

THEN WHAT IS CLIMATE?

The difference between weather and climate is that weather consists of the short-term changes in the atmosphere, from minutes to months long. Climate, however, is the average of weather over time and space. An easy way to remember the difference is that climate is what you expect, like a very hot summer, and weather is what you get, like a hot day with pop-up thunderstorms.

CLIMATE ALWAYS CHANGES

Earth's climate is always changing. In the past, Earth's climate has gone through warmer and cooler periods, each lasting thousands of years. The climate of a city, region or the entire planet changes very slowly. These changes take place on the scale of tens, hundreds and thousands of years.

Climate change is a change in the typical or average weather of a region or city. This could be a change in a region's average annual rainfall, for example. Or it could be a change in a city's average temperature for a given month or season. Climate change is also a change in Earth's overall climate. This could be a change in Earth's average temperature, for example. Or it could be a change in Earth's typical precipitation patterns.

AN AURA OF CLIMATE SCIENCE

Human activity is altering two of our atmosphere's protective duties. The stratospheric ozone layer—the part of the atmosphere that protects us from the sun's ultraviolet radiation—has deteriorated. And the increasing level of "greenhouse gases" in the atmosphere is raising Earth's temperature faster than at any time in the past.

The Aura Earth-observing satellite launched in July 2004 is the latest in a line of instruments and satellites that give us the ability to measure changes in climate and air quality and in the health of the ozone layer that protects living things from UV radiation.

PLANTING CLIMATE IDEAS

Through photosynthesis, plants use carbon dioxide to make oxygen and help regulate the amount of both gases in the atmosphere. Since plants grow faster and use more carbon dioxide when carbon dioxide levels are high, some people believe that plants can absorb much of the excess carbon dioxide produced by burning fossil fuels.

Few places on the earth have not been affected by the influence of humans. The degree of that influence varies a great deal from place to place, but in the mid-Atlantic region it has a long history. This area was changed many thousands of years ago by Native Americans and since the mid-1600's by colonial settlers. The lands now covered with forest at Smithsonian Environmental Research Center (SERC) are no exception to this.

A 2010 study shows that forests in the eastern United States are growing at a faster rate than at any time in the last 225 years. The chief reason researchers say, appears to be climate change, specifically: rising levels of atmospheric carbon dioxide, higher temperatures, and longer growing seasons.

During the past 22 years CO2 levels at SERC have risen 12%, the mean temperature has increased by nearly three-tenths of a degree and the growing season has lengthened by 7.8 days. The trees now have more CO2 and an extra week to put on weight.

TRUE OR FALSE

43

INVISIBLE SUNLIGHT

Sunlight, like all light, consists of energy that moves through the air in the form of waves in different sizes, or wavelengths. The light you can see is the visible spectrum. Invisible ultraviolet waves have shorter wavelengths and more energy than visible light.

Ultraviolet radiation (UV) is, at least to humans, an invisible part of sunlight. But as you well know from a sunny day at the beach, it's biologically very active. UV radiation can have severe effects on exposed skin and eyes, cause cancer, weaken immune systems, and affect plants, animals, and ecosystems.

About 95 percent of the UV light that passes through the ozone layer gives you a suntan. It's called UVA. The other five percent, known as UVB, gives you a sunburn. Exposure to UVB in sunlight can alter the DNA in your body's skin cells and increase the risk that they will become cancerous years later. UVA causes skin to age and wrinkle and may affect the development of skin cancer, too. UV light can also cause cataracts to form over the lenses of the eye.

The amount of UV radiation reaching the Earth's surface varies widely around the globe and through time. The amount of UV that reaches the ground is mainly affected by:

ELEVATION   **CLOUDS**   **OZONE**

Atop a 120-foot tower, Smithsonian Environmental Research Center scientists study UV every day. A disk with 18 different filters rotates 15 times every minute. The filters select different UV wavelengths, which are passed to a sensor and recording computer. The sensor is kept dry and at a constant temperature to get a stable response. Smithsonian Institution scientists pioneered atmospheric monitoring in the late 1800s.

TRUE or FALSE

False   True

HERO UP HIGH, VILLAIN NEARBY

In the stratosphere, ozone protects us, absorbing much of the sun's harmful ultraviolet radiation. But at ground level, in the troposphere, carried in the air we breathe, ozone is a poison that burns and corrodes living and non-living things. Small amounts of ozone develop naturally, especially during lightning storms, but spew industrial chemicals and automobile exhausts into the atmosphere, cook them with heat and sunlight, and ozone levels can rise dangerously high. Ozone is the main component of "photochemical smog."

GOLDILOCKS AND THE THREE OZONE LAYERS

TOO HIGH	JUST RIGHT	TOO LOW

HISTORY OF OZONE

Take a deep breath! Oxygen is reactive and likes to combine with other molecules. This reactivity enables people and most other living things to turn the food they eat into energy (metabolism), with carbon dioxide and water as byproducts.

Troposphere

Stratosphere

Mesosphere

Thermosphere

18   48   90   350

Christian Friedrich Schoenbein discovered ozone in 1839 while he was a professor in Switzerland. He took advantage of ozone's reactivity to develop a way to measure the presence of ozone and demonstrate that it occurs in the atmosphere. Schoenbein used a mixture of starch, potassium iodide, and water spread on filter paper, like you find in a coffeemaker or an air filter. The paper, named Schoenbein paper after its creator, changes color when there's ozone in the air, staining the paper purple. The darker the color, the more ozone present.

OZONE IN THE NO-ZONE

Ozone reacts with living tissue. In plants, ozone can hamper photosynthesis and lower crop yield. In people, ozone can inflame delicate tissues in the lungs, leaving them open to asthma and infections. Children and elderly people are especially at risk from ozone exposure. Kids breathe relatively more air than adults and are more affected by surface ozone.

The Environmental Protection Agency has established an ozone standard to protect humans and plants from ozone effects. However, there is evidence to suggest that this standard, based on human studies, is not protective of very sensitive plant species. These plants may still be harmed at ozone levels below the standard.

KEEPING THE TEMPO

What's in the air we breathe? NASA's TEMPO (Tropospheric Emissions: Monitoring Pollution) program aims to answer this question with more detail and precision than ever before, by taking atmospheric chemistry measurements from space. TEMPO will be the first space-based instrument to monitor major air pollutants across the North American continent every daylight hour at high resolution. The instrument, a UV and visible-light spectrometer, will hitch a ride on a commercial satellite to an orbit about 22,000 miles above Earth's equator. This will enable TEMPO to monitor daily variations in ozone, nitrogen dioxide, and other air pollution from the Atlantic to the Pacific, and from Mexico to Canada, with far better detail.

TRUE
OR
FALSE

TRUE

FALSE

SOMETHING (ELSE)

Unhealthy air leads to many deaths worldwide each year. According to the World Health Organization, 2.4 million deaths each year are directly attributable to air pollution. Ozone isn't the only traveling pollutant. Air pollution includes toxic gases and fine particles or aerosols. High concentrations of ozone and fine aerosols are the leading causes of air pollution-related illness and death.

ACID RAIN'S POISON COCKTAIL

A team of archaeologists, architects, ironworkers, and marble cutters has just started a new project. Its goal? To restore the Temple of Athena, a masterpiece of Greek architecture that was built in the fifth century B.C. The surface of the historic monument has been deteriorating for decades. It's time for temple-saving action.

These buildings, like many monuments, are built of marble—one of the hardest stones. Why are they in need of restoration? Wind and rain have always had an effect on buildings, but the main cause of deterioration is pollution. The problem is not just in Athens. In cities around the world, historic buildings are literally being dissolved away.

The major culprits are acid rain and smog (visible as a reddish brown haze), which is a problem in most of the world's large cities. Both originate with the burning of fossil fuels, such as coal and petroleum.

IN THE AIR

All rain is slightly acidic, but acid rain does much more damage to buildings. It is especially harmful to buildings made from rocks that contain calcium carbonate or magnesium carbonate. Marble, used in many Athenian buildings, and the softer, even more vulnerable, limestone both contain carbonates.

Until the source of the pollution is completely removed, any efforts to restore ancient buildings will be only stopgap measures. The team of workers on the Acropolis in Athens, in other words, is dealing with the symptoms, but not the cure.

In many countries, fossil-fuel-burning power plants and other industrial plants now remove some acidic gases from the waste products that would otherwise be dispersed through smokestacks. Also, special devices are being fitted to car tailpipes to remove some of these gases from exhaust fumes.

BLACK CARBON

Black carbon is the fancy name for soot. And like carbon dioxide, it's causing changes in the Arctic climate. The light color of snow and ice reflects most of the Sun's energy back into space, rather than being absorbed by the dark color of land and open water. That is one reason the Arctic's cold is so extreme—and our planet does not overheat.

Aerosol is the overall term for very small atmospheric particles. To be called an aerosol, the particle size should be less than one tenth the thickness of a human hair! Aerosols have complex effects on Earth's climate. In general, they tend to cool the surface by reflecting radiation from the sun back into space. But some aerosols, such as dust and smoke, absorb solar radiation and heat the atmosphere where they are concentrated.

OTHER POLLUTANTS

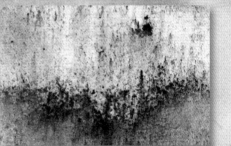

CARBON DIOXIDE

CARBON MONOXIDE

NITROGEN OXIDES

SULFUR DIOXIDE

OTHER AEROSOLS

TRUE or FALSE

TRUE   FALSE

WEATHER OR NOT

Imagine a rotating sphere that is 8000 miles in diameter, has a bumpy surface, is surrounded by a 25-mile-deep mixture of different gases whose concentrations vary in space and over time, and is heated, along with its surrounding gases, by a nuclear reactor 93 million miles away. Then, imagine that after watching the gaseous mixture, you are expected to predict what happens in one tiny place on the sphere — one, two, or more days into the future. This is the job of a weather forecaster.

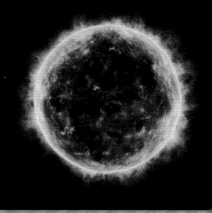

AGES OF WEATHER WATCHING

The art of weather forecasting began when early groups of humans used repeating events to help them keep track of seasonal changes in the weather. Throughout the centuries, attempts have been made to produce forecasts based on **weather lore** and personal observations.

By the 1600s, early scientists understood that more knowledge was necessary to understand the atmosphere. In order to find this knowledge, scientists needed instruments to measure the properties of the atmosphere, such as moisture, temperature, and pressure.

JOSEPH HENRY'S OBSERVERS

Can you imagine a time when weather forecasts were not available, or when people did not know that storms followed predictable paths? The science of meteorology was brand new when the Smithsonian was founded in 1846, but over the next 30 years, the Institution developed a national network for collecting weather data, and made possible some of the earliest weather forecasts.

Joseph Henry wanted a consistent way to watch the weather and begin "solving the problem of American storms." It was not yet known, for example, that many North American storms moved from west to east. The Smithsonian's network of volunteer observers eventually grew to over six hundred people across the US as well as Latin America and the Caribbean.

TRUE or FALSE   T   F

OCEAN AIR

Even if you've never gone to a beach to watch a sunrise or sunset or to ride the waves, the oceans probably affected you as recently as this morning — when you may have checked the weather and decided what to wear. The atmosphere and the ocean interact to produce weather. Moist air develops over warm water. Dry air develops over cool water.

CONVECTION

SEA BREEZE

LAND BREEZE

WHAT'S AN EL NIÑO?

An El Niño (Spanish for "the boy child") occurs when the atmosphere and ocean waters interact to form warmer than normal water in the eastern and central Pacific Ocean. Sometimes an El Niño is followed by a La Niña whose effects on weather patterns are generally opposite to those caused by an El Niño.

El Niño events have occurred for tens of thousands of years. But they happen at irregular intervals, and their intensity varies from event to event. Every three to seven years, a large-scale El Niño occurs that has impacts beyond coastal Peru. This global event is also called El Niño.

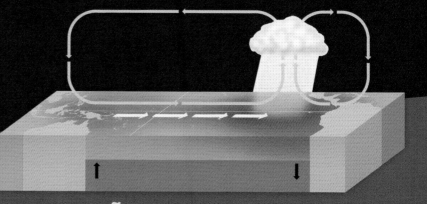

EL NIÑO CONDITIONS

CURRENT AFFAIRS

Winds in the atmosphere drive surface currents that move warm water from the equator to the poles and cold water from the poles to the equator — setting up nearly circular patterns of movement.

Ocean currents have several different causes, many of which are due to changes in density. Some ocean currents are convection currents. Convection currents like this also take place in the atmosphere. We encounter these convection currents as wind.

False

True

TRUE or FALSE

THE LIGHT OF DAY

In the complex recipe of Earth's climate and weather, no ingredient is more important than the Sun. Without its intense energy, life on our planet would be impossible. At an average distance of 93 million miles, only half of one billionth of the Sun's energy reaches Earth. yet even that fraction of the Sun's power is massive — totaling more than 300,000 times the electrical generating capacity of the United States!

THE SUN-WEATHER CONNECTION

The energy that the Earth receives from the Sun is the basic cause of our changing weather. Solar heat warms the huge air masses that make up large and small weather systems. The day-night and summer-winter cycles in the weather have obvious causes and effects. Are there other, less obvious ways in which the Sun affects weather and climate? Because of absorption and scattering of sunlight in the Earth's atmosphere, these measurements are unreliable if made from the ground. Recently, techniques have been developed to measure the solar constant from space vehicles.

A BEND OF LIGHT

REFRACTION

The bending of light by a lens or by the atmosphere is an example of refraction. Refraction happens because of change of the speed of light as it moves from one medium to another, such as from air to glass, or through air which is changing in density. The path taken by a ray of light is the path that takes the least time.

MIRAGE

INVISIBILITY

TWINKLING

BLACK HOLE

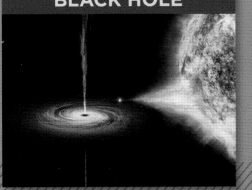

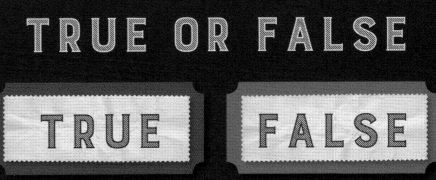

TRUE OR FALSE

TRUE   FALSE

WEATHER TOPICS

To a certain extent, Earth's climate has always changed. The difference today is that it is changing faster than ever before. And humanity wields enormous power to influence the planet's future—so much that some scholars have taken to calling this age the Anthropocene, or the Epoch of Man.

AN IMPERFECT STORM

The Arctic's climate has been changing. Spring thaws are earlier. Fall freeze-ups are later. Sea ice is shrinking. Unfamiliar species of plants and animals are appearing. Intense storms are more frequent. Ice and snow reflect about 85–90% of sunlight. Open ocean water reflects just 10%. But with less ice cover, the ocean and the land warm up, causing more ice to melt, further warming the planet.

Even if storms do not become stronger or more frequent, their impacts could. Increasingly, Arctic coastal communities risk more flooding and erosion when a storm hits. The first line of defense against waves—sea ice and permafrost—has weakened as the Arctic's climate has warmed.

The United States set records in 2011 and 2012 for the number of weather disasters that exceeded $1 billion in losses. Most were storms. All of these weather events have happened as the concentration of greenhouse gases in the atmosphere has been rising higher than it has been for at least 100,000 years.

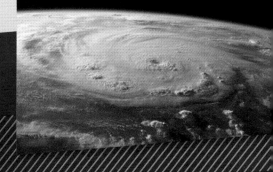

False
True

TRUE or FALSE

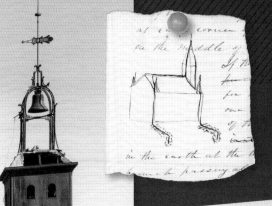

LIGHTNING STRIKES

Joseph Henry, the first Secretary of the Smithsonian, was as important to the study of lightning as he was to the study of all weather. He admired Benjamin Franklin for finding ways to protect houses and other buildings "from the lightnings of the heavens."

Lightning was among the many scientific topics on which Joseph Henry was considered an expert during his lifetime. Henry's research in this area and his efforts to protect buildings from lightning show us a point he proved throughout his life: that the scientific knowledge gained from basic research was essential for solving real-world problems.

WIND EROSION

Erosion is the process of wearing down an object by various forces. We can see the process of erosion all around us in small pillars of dust left behind after a rainstorm, in the fanciful shapes left in a melting snowbank, in the smooth shape of a mound of dirt that is gradually spreading out, or in ditches carved in soft ground after a rainstorm.

Erosion also occurs on very small scales. Scientists and engineers use beams of energetic particles in a controlled erosion process to create microscopic structures for smart phones, and other nano-technology devices.

LEARNING ABOUT
SOUND

The Smithsonian's National Museum of American History houses literally millions of objects which preserve and illustrate our nation's rich history. Among the many stories that these objects tell are the ways that Americans have learned about science. Let's explore a unique and beautiful collection of instruments used to teach acoustics, the science of sound. These historic instruments were designed to be engaging and to challenge students to think in new ways about the physical world.

HEARING SOUNDS

One of nature's greatest wonders is the ability of the human ear to distinguish among the millions of sounds around us. All sounds have characteristic qualities which your ear learns to recognize. We have no difficulty telling apart a factory whistle, a soprano singer, and a piano, even when they have the same pitch.

WAVE MACHINE

In the 19th century, teaching the principles of waves became one of the basic goals of the science classroom. And since most waves are too fast to see directly, a variety of wave models and machines were developed to imitate them. Compared to other kinds of waves, sound waves are simple and can used to demonstrate nearly all the properties of waves.

Wave machines and wave models began to appear in science classrooms around the middle of the 19th century. They were used to teach the idea of waves, which were central to a new understanding of the physical world that we now refer to as "classical physics." Classical physics includes many subjects — acoustics, heat, light and, later, electricity and even magnetism — all of which could be explained in terms of different kinds of waves.

If set in vibration and left by itself, a sound source will continue to vibrate freely and produce a tone of constant frequency which will gradually die away as the vibrating energy dissipates. For example, a tuning fork struck and left by itself makes several tones, but within a few seconds only the fundamental tone can be heard. A tuning fork makes practically a pure tone. That is, the vibrations are of only one frequency and they have a smooth regular waveform. Sounds from other sources such as musical instruments, the human voice, or noises have waveforms that are less smooth and more complicated.

By the last decades of the 19th century, tuning forks were among the most precise of all scientific instruments. Specialized techniques were developed to use them for measuring different kinds of vibrations, and they were frequently used as high-precision timing standards. Albert Michelson used light reflected from the vibrating tines of a tuning fork to make a historic measurements of the speed of light.

Sound Distractions

TRUE or FALSE | TRUE | FALSE

SOUND OR MUSIC?

The sounds to which our ears respond may be classified as either music or noise: the sound of a harp, the song of a bird, even the sharp whistle of a tugboat can all be classified as music.

LOUD OR INTENSE?

How loud is a sound? It's apparent that one noise is louder than another, but how much louder? And how can we measure it?